EARTH'S LAST FRONTIERS

ARCTIC TUNDRA

Ellen Labrecque

Raintree

Raintree is an imprint of Capstone Global Library Limited, a company incorporated in England and Wales having its registered office at 7 Pilgrim Street, London, EC4V 6LB – Registered company number: 6695582

www.raintreepublishers.co.uk
myorders@raintreepublishers.co.uk

Text © Capstone Global Library Limited 2014
First published in hardback in 2014
The moral rights of the proprietor have been asserted.

Edited by Rebecca Rissman, Dan Nunn, and Adrian Vigliano
Designed by Tim Bond
Picture research by Liz Alexander
Originated by Capstone Global Library Ltd
Printed in China by CTPS

ISBN 978 1 406 27167 6
17 16 15 14 13
10 9 8 7 6 5 4 3 2 1

British Library Cataloguing in Publication Data
Labrecque, Ellen.
Arctic tundra. – (Earth's last frontiers)
A full catalogue record for this book is available from the British Library.

Acknowledgements

We would like to thank the following for permission to reproduce photographs:

Alamy pp. 15 (© Kevin Schafer), 26 (© David Newham); Corbis pp. 7 (© Alexandra Kobalenko/All Canada Photos), 11 (© Geray Sweeney), 17 (© Staffan Widstrand), 18 (© Buff & Gerald Corsi/Visuals Unlimited), 19 (© Wayne Lynch/All Canada Photos), 23 (© Fred Hirschmann/Science Faction); FLPA p. 21 (© Jim Brandenburg/Minden Pictures); Getty Images pp. 24 (Burgess Blevins/Taxi), 25 (The Asahi Shimbun Premium via Getty Images); NASA p. 4; Nature Picture Library pp. 12 (© Bryan and Cherry Alexander), 29 (© Jeff Turner); Science Photo Library p. 27 (David Hay Jones); Shutterstock pp. 5 (© Wild Arctic Pictures), 6 (© Wild Arctic Pictures), 16 (© George Burba), 20 (© Sergey Krasnoshchokov), 22 (© Karin Wassmer), 28 (© Ekaterina Baranova); SuperStock pp. 8 (John E Marriott / All Canada Photos), 9 (Wayne Lynch / All Canada Photos), 10 (Biosphoto), 13 (Juniors), 14 (Stellar Stock); Design features courtesy of Shutterstock (© newyear), (© Zlatko Guzmic).

Cover photograph of a tundra landscape reproduced with permission of Nature Picture Library (© Jeff Wilson).

Every effort has been made to contact copyright holders of material reproduced in this book. Any omissions will be rectified in subsequent printings if notice is given to the publisher.

All the internet addresses (URLs) given in this book were valid at the time of going to press. However, due to the dynamic nature of the internet, some addresses may have changed, or sites may have changed or ceased to exist since publication. While the author and publisher regret any inconvenience this may cause readers, no responsibility for any such changes can be accepted by either the author or the publisher.

CONTENTS

A FINAL FRONTIER

The Arctic tundra has one of the coldest and windiest **climates** on Earth. It is very hard for people to get there. It is even harder to survive the climate once they arrive! Let's take a look at this freezing frontier.

WOW!

The tundra is considered one of the coldest **biomes**, or places to live, in the entire world!

WHAT IS THE ARCTIC TUNDRA?

The Arctic tundra surrounds the **North Pole**. The word *tundra* means "treeless wasteland". The Arctic tundra is so cold and windy that trees are not able to grow here.

WOW!

Winds blow across the Arctic tundra at up to 97 kilometres (60 miles) per hour. This is as fast as a car on the motorway.

WHY IS THE ARCTIC TUNDRA UNEXPLORED?

The tundra is difficult to explore because it is covered in snow and ice most of the year. Temperatures drop far below freezing. And, for many weeks during the winter, the sun does not appear at all.

WOW!

The coldest temperature ever recorded in the Arctic is −68 degrees Celsius (−90 degrees Fahrenheit).

ARCTIC TUNDRA ZONES

The Arctic tundra has three different areas. The low Arctic tundra has permafrost with top layers of ground that melt during the summer. This region has the most plant life.

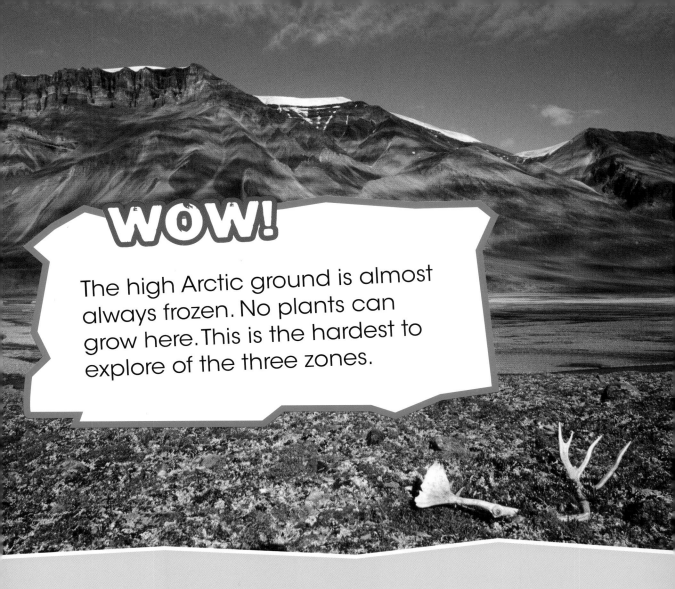

WOW!

The high Arctic ground is almost always frozen. No plants can grow here. This is the hardest to explore of the three zones.

The middle Arctic tundra has less plant life, and the ground stays frozen longer. The high Arctic tundra has the harshest climate of all.

WINTER

During the cold winter months, explorers battle fierce winds. The winds blow up snow into drifts that grow taller month after month, and year after year. The drifts make it even harder to travel from place to place.

WOW!

The Arctic tundra only gets as much rainfall as a **desert** each year. But, because it is so cold, most of the snow never melts.

SUMMER

In the summer, parts of the tundra get sunlight 24 hours a day. Temperatures rise as high as 10 degrees Celsius (50 degrees Fahrenheit). Lakes and pools form from melted ice and snow. But the land cannot absorb the water because of the permafrost.

WOW!

The freezing and melting of the land makes the tundra lumpy and full of deep cracks. The ground becomes difficult to travel over.

THE LANDSCAPE

During the summer, water soaks the ground and ponds form. During the winter, the ground freezes and cracks open. The cracks make it dangerous to walk across the land.

WOW!

Pingos, or oval hills, cover the tundra. Pingos form because large amounts of water freeze under the ground surface. The frozen water pushes the land up to form a hill.

PLANTS

Few plants grow in the Arctic tundra because there is not enough sunlight. The plants that do grow have shallow roots because the frozen ground keeps deep roots from growing.

WOW!

There are only about 1,700 different plants that grow in the Arctic. Over the whole of Earth, there are 176 times this many.

ANIMALS

Few animals live in the Arctic tundra year-round. Some animals, such as the caribou, make the Arctic tundra their summer home. During the winter, they **migrate** south to a warmer place.

WOW!

Most animals on the Arctic tundra will not attack people unless they are frightened. Still, explorers always have to stay on guard against wildlife.

THE LIGHT SHOW

Explorers who arrive in the Arctic tundra during the winter enjoy a natural light show. The northern lights, or the **aurora borealis**, appear as a curtain of multicoloured lights hanging in the dark sky.

WOW!

The northern lights are created by particles from the sun reacting with Earth's atmosphere. They are like nature's own fireworks!

PEOPLE ON THE TUNDRA

Some groups of people live in the Arctic tundra. The **Inuits** live mostly on the coastal areas. They survive by hunting for seals, whales, and polar bears. Because few plants grow here, their diet is almost all meat.

WOW!

The town of Siorapaluk, Greenland, is the most northern village in the world. Seventy people live there and survive by hunting and fishing. They travel around on sledges pulled by dogs!

HOW WE EXPLORE

Research centres in the Arctic tundra allow scientists to live in this extreme habitat. They explore by riding on snowmobiles and sledges throughout the region.

WOW!

In 2010, scientists uncovered the remains of the most ancient polar bear ever found. It was frozen deep in the ground. They believe the bear lived about 120,000 years ago.

27

ONLY IN THE ARCTIC TUNDRA

The Arctic tundra is changing every day because of **global warming**. Some animals have moved from warmer climates onto the tundra. Animals now fight for food and land space.

The Arctic tundra is a dark and mysterious world for much of the year. The extreme cold makes it a place that only few will ever explore.

GLOSSARY

aurora borealis colourful lights that appear in the night sky in the Northern Hemisphere

biome large area, including the plants and animals that live there

climate what the weather is like in a certain area over time

desert very dry land covered in sand

global warming gradual increase in the temperature of Earth's atmosphere

Inuit group of native Arctic people

migrate move from one region to another

North Pole northernmost point on Earth

pingo dome-shaped mound made of a layer of soil over a large core of ice

FIND OUT MORE

There are lots of sources with information about the Arctic tundra! You can start with these books and websites.

BOOKS

Arctic and Antarctic, Philip Steele (Kingfisher, 2013)

Expedition to the Arctic (Travelling Wild), Alex Woolf (Wayland, 2013)

WEBSITES

www.bbc.co.uk/nature/habitats/Polar_region

See some fantastic Arctic videos on the BBC's nature website.

gowild.wwf.org.uk/polar

Learn more about the Arctic on WWF's website.

INDEX